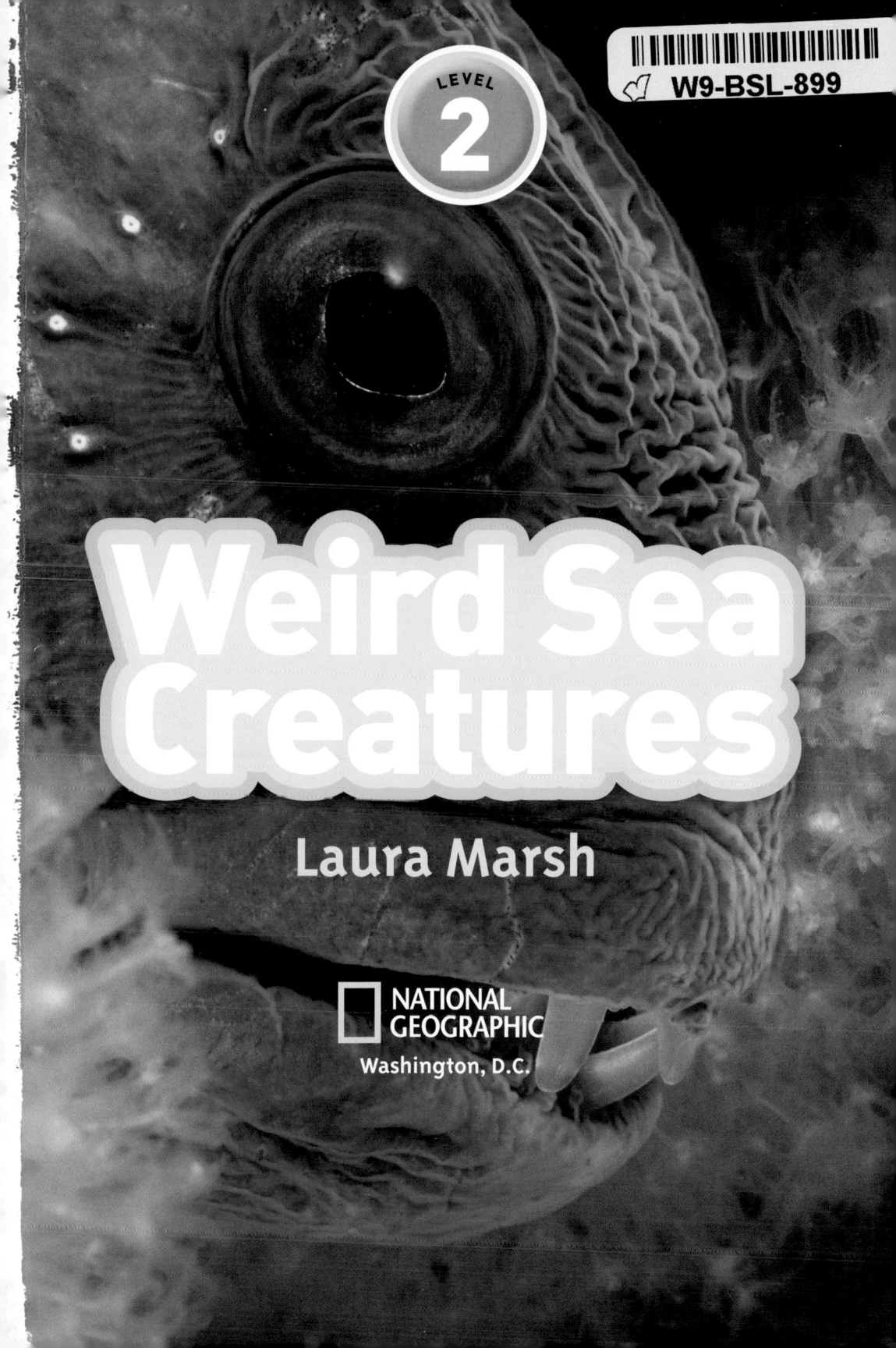
LEVEL
2
W9-BSL-899
Weird Sea Creatures
Laura Marsh
NATIONAL GEOGRAPHIC
Washington, D.C.

**For Finn and Zoë**

**—L. F. M.**

National Geographic gratefully acknowledges the assistance of the National Aquarium.

This material is based upon work supported by the National Science Foundation under Grant No. DRL-1114251. Any opinions, findings, and conclusions or recommendations expressed in this material are those of the author(s) and do not necessarily reflect the views of the National Science Foundation.

As seen on the National Geographic Channel

Copyright © 2012 National Geographic Society
Published by the National Geographic Society, Washington, D.C. 20036. All rights reserved.
Reproduction in whole or in part without written permission of the publisher is prohibited.

Design by YAY! Design

Paperback ISBN: 978-1-4263-1047-8
Library edition ISBN: 978-1-4263-1048-5

Photo credits

Cover, Charles Hood/Oceans Image/Photoshot; 1, © Espen Rekdal/SeaPics.com; 4, Ocean/Corbis; 6, Jim Watt/Perspectives/Getty Images; 8, David Shale/naturepl.com; 9 (top), Michael Patrick O'Neill/National Geographic Your Shot; 9 (bottom), Scott Costa/National Geographic Your Shot; 11, Stephen Frink/Science Faction/Getty Images; 13, Norbert Wu/Minden Pictures/National Geographic Stock; 14, Jason Edwards/National Geographic Stock; 15, Visuals Unlimited/Corbis; 16, Norbert Wu/Minden Pictures/National Geographic Stock; 18 (bottom), Bill Curtsinger/National Geographic Stock; 18 (top), Dorling Kindersley RF/Getty Images; 19, Norbert Wu/Minden Pictures/National Geographic Stock; 20, Jeffrey de Guzman/National Geographic Your Shot; 22, David Doubilet/National Geographic Stock; 23, Howard St. Quintin/National Geographic Your Shot; 24, Dordo Bmobic/National Geographic Your Shot; 25 (inset), Norbert Wu/Science Faction/Corbis; 27, Emory Kristof/National Geographic Stock; 28, Kerryn Parkinson/© NORFANZ founding parties; 29, Susan Dabritz/SeaPics.com; 30 (top), Jason Edwards/National Geographic Stock; 30 (center), Emory Kristof/National Geographic Stock; 30 (bottom), Scott Costa/National Geographic Your Shot; 31 (top left), Jeffrey de Guzman/National Geographic Your Shot; 31 (top right), Jon Milnes/Shutterstock; 31 (bottom left), zebra0209/Shutterstock; 31 (bottom right), Colin Parker/National Geographic Your Shot; 32 (center left), Stephen Frink/Digital Vision/Getty Images; 32 (top left), Jason Edwards/National Geographic Stock; 32 (top right), Michael Patrick O'Neill/National Geographic Your Shot; 32 (bottom right), Jeffrey de Guzman/National Geographic Your Shot; 32 (bottom left), Emory Kristof/National Geographic Stock; 32 (center right), Norbert Wu/Minden Pictures/National Geographic Stock

National Geographic supports K–12 educators with ELA Common Core Resources.
Visit natgeoed.org/commoncore for more information.

Printed in the United States of America
Paperback: 14/WOR/4
RLB: 14/WOR/2

# Table of Contents

Strange But True . . . . . 4

Survival Skills . . . . . 6

Hide and Seek . . . . . 10

Big Eyes . . . . . 12

Making Light . . . . . 14

Expert Food Finders . . . . . 16

Deadly Dangers . . . . . 20

Strange Senses . . . . . 24

Super Subs! . . . . . 26

Stump Your Parents . . . . . 30

Glossary . . . . . 32

# Strange But True

balloonfish

Many strange sea creatures live in the ocean.

Some are beautiful. Some are ugly. Some are cute, and some are scary.

Weird sea creatures are strange for a reason. The funny way they look and the strange things they do help them live in the ocean.

# Survival Skills

Snorkeling in shallow water

diagonal butterflyfish

Some sea animals live in the shallow ocean waters. Some live in the deep ocean.

The ocean can be a hard place to live. Deep areas are cold and dark. It can be hard to find food.

And the ocean can be dangerous. There are many predators. Any animal can quickly become dinner for another animal.

**Water Word**

**PREDATOR: An animal that hunts and eats other animals**

Sea creatures have special skills that help them find food. They also have strange body parts that can help them hide and stay safe from other animals.

How weird are these sea creatures? Let's find out!

A Dumbo octopus finds food on the ocean floor with its large eyes.

A leafy sea dragon blends in with the seaweed around it.

A moray eel's sharp teeth catch prey.

# Hide and Seek

Camouflage (KAM-uh-flazh) helps animals hide from their enemies. Looking strange helps them blend in to the plants or water around them.

Camouflage also helps animals catch dinner. Do you see the stonefish in the picture? Most fish don't because it looks like rock or coral. When they swim too close, the stonefish springs from the ocean floor. It grabs dinner in a flash.

**Water Word**

**CAMOUFLAGE: An animal's natural color or form that blends in with what is around it**

**Q** What is the strongest sea creature?

**A** A mussel!

# Big Eyes

The deep ocean gets very little light. Many animals that live there have large eyes. Big eyes help creatures see in the darkness and find prey.

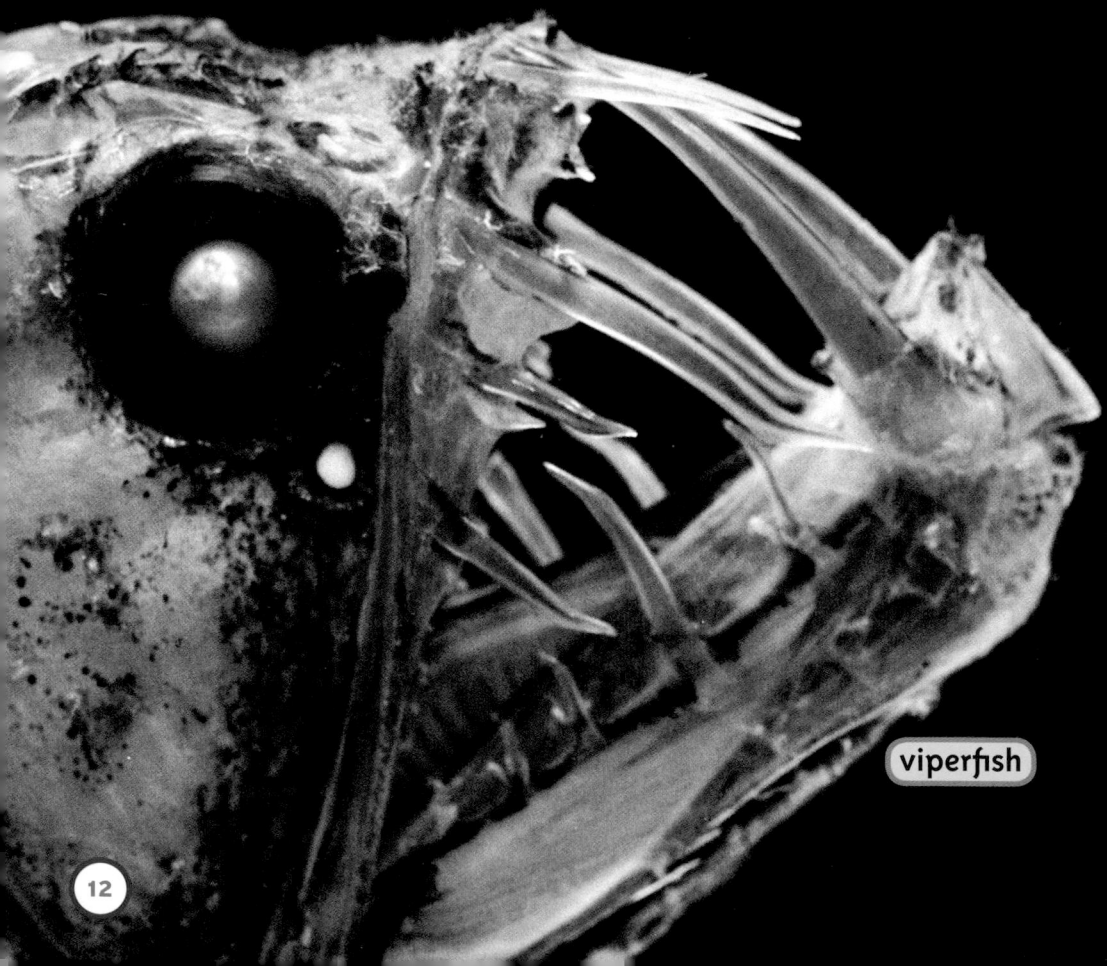

viperfish

This viperfish used its big eyes to spot a hatchetfish. Dinnertime!

The hatchetfish uses its own large eyes to find tiny shrimp to eat in the dark sea.

**Water Word**

**PREY:** An animal that is eaten by another animal

# Making Light

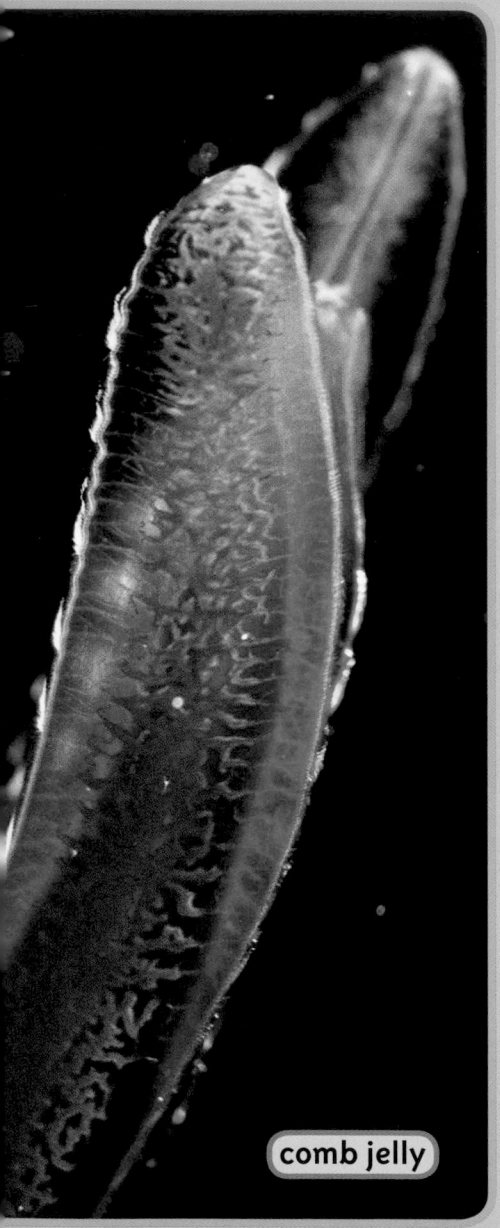
comb jelly

Many creatures in the deep, dark sea have a special trick—they make their own light! This is called bioluminescence (BYE-oh-loom-i-NESS-ants).

**Water Word**

**BIOLUMINESCENCE:** Light that an animal makes by itself

Some sea creatures use their own light as a flashlight to find prey. Light can draw prey toward an animal, too. And light can surprise enemies, so an animal can make a quick escape.

# Expert Food Finders

Some animals have wacky body parts that help them catch meals.

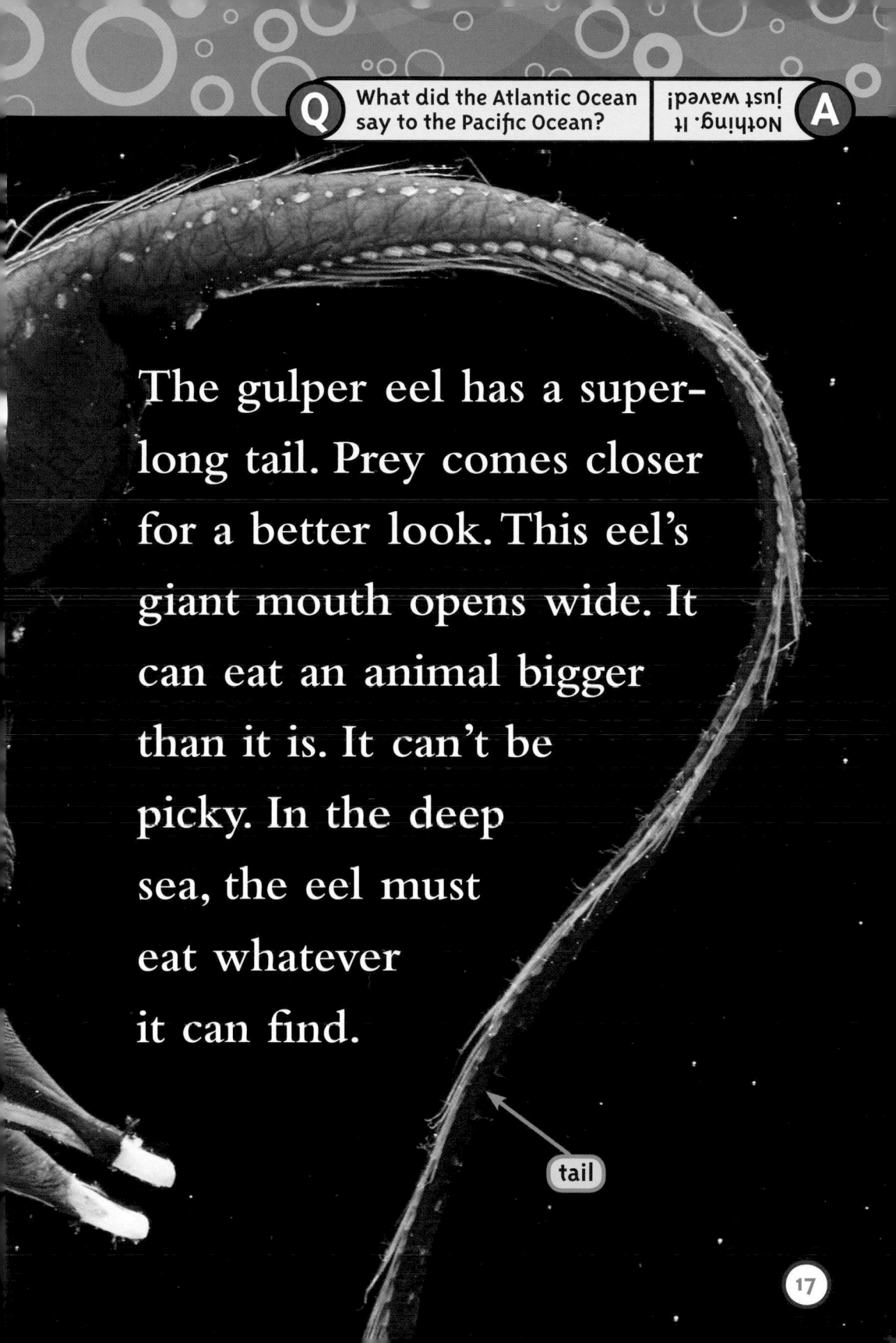


**Q** What did the Atlantic Ocean say to the Pacific Ocean?

**A** Nothing. It just waved!

The gulper eel has a super-long tail. Prey comes closer for a better look. This eel's giant mouth opens wide. It can eat an animal bigger than it is. It can't be picky. In the deep sea, the eel must eat whatever it can find.

The tiny cookie-cutter shark locks onto its prey with strange sucking lips. Its sharp teeth sink in. They leave a bite the shape of a circle.

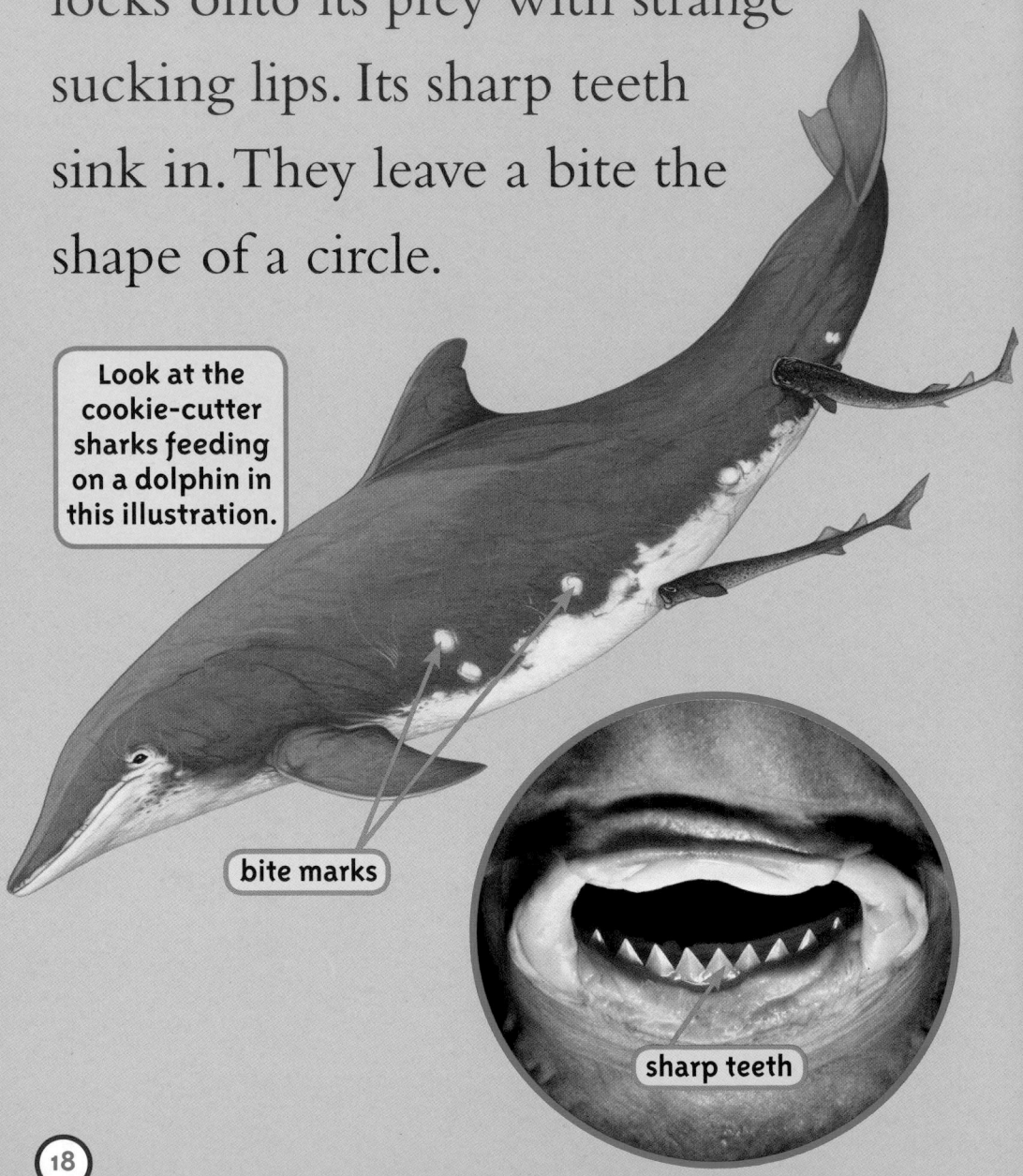

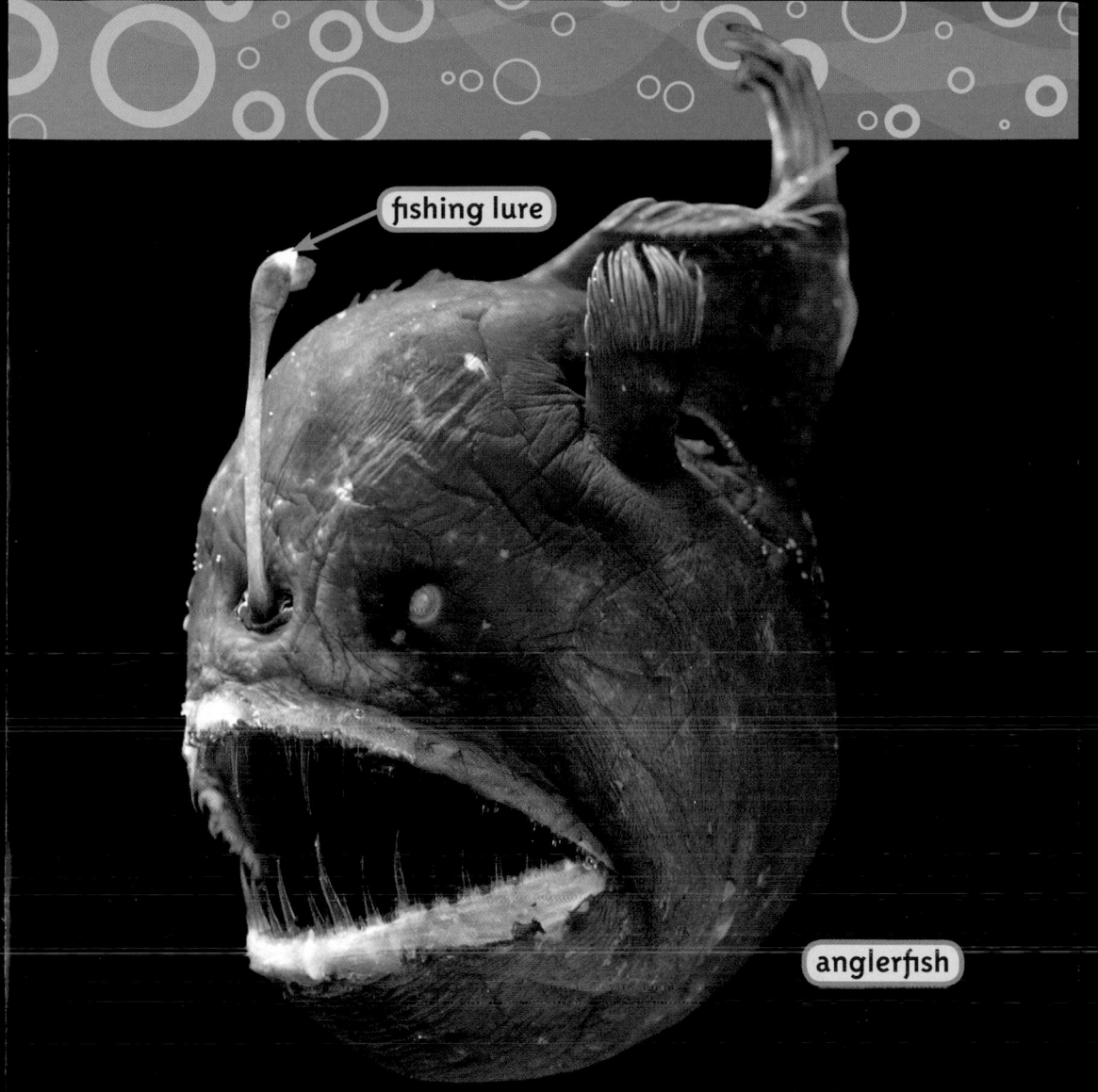


An anglerfish has its own fishing pole called a lure. The lure glows, and other fish want to know what it is. When they get close, the anglerfish eats them.

# Deadly Dangers

Bumping into some sea creatures can be bad news.

The yellow sea anemone (ah-NEM-oh-nee) looks like a pretty flower. But it has stinging parts that have deadly venom. When a fish is stung, its muscles stop working. Then the anemone eats the fish.

**Water Word**

**VENOM:** A liquid some animals make that can cause stinging, pain, or death

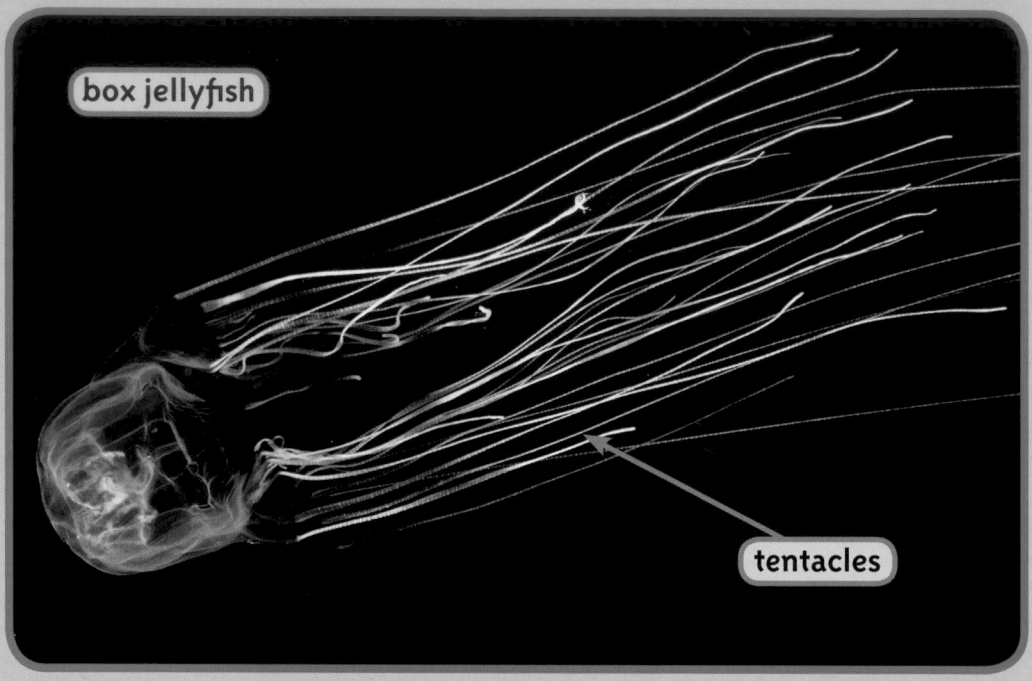


The box jellyfish is one of the most dangerous animals in the world. It has arms called tentacles (TEN-tah-kullz) that grow up to ten feet long. The tentacles deliver a painful, deadly sting.

Q What sea creature goes well with toast?

A A jellyfish!

This lionfish has crazy spiky fins. But you wouldn't want to touch them. The fins on its back are sharp and can sting you.

# Strange Senses

Some animals near the ocean floor don't even have eyes! They can't see their food. So they use other senses to find it.

A sea cucumber can feel tiny pieces of food stuck to its tube feet. It curls its feet in and licks them clean.

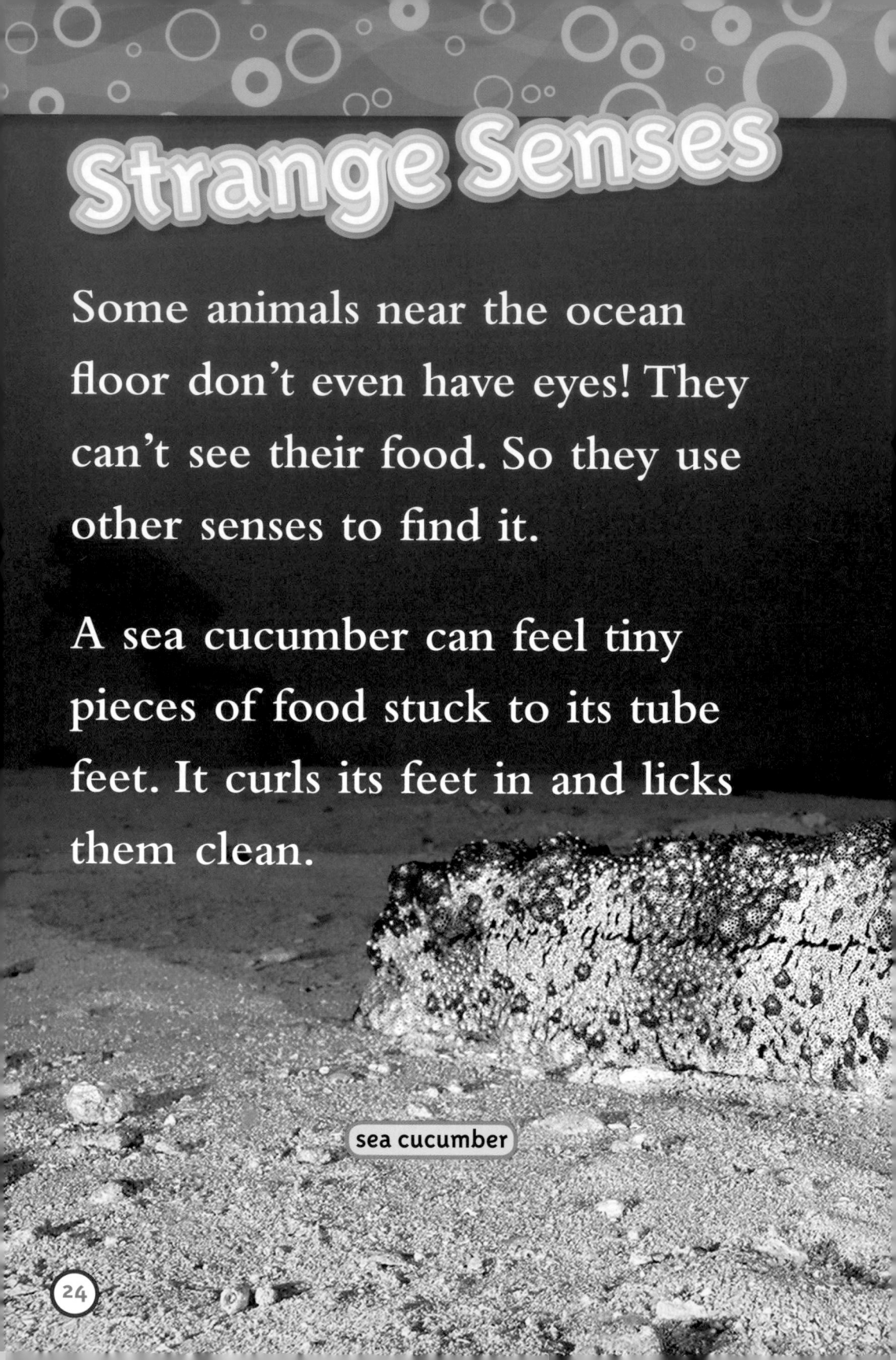

sea cucumber

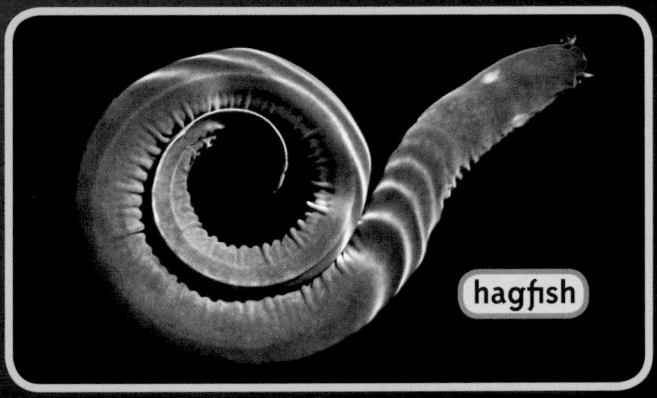


A hagfish has a super strong sense of smell and touch. It can smell food that's fallen from higher up in the ocean. It also uses feelers to find meals.

# Super Subs!

How do we know about weird sea creatures in the deep ocean?

People can't dive deep to see these strange creatures. It's too cold and dark there. And the water pressure is strong enough to crush a person.

But humans can use machines called submersibles (sub-MER-sih-bullz) to explore the deep ocean.

Sometimes people control them from far away, like a remote-controlled car. And sometimes people ride inside.

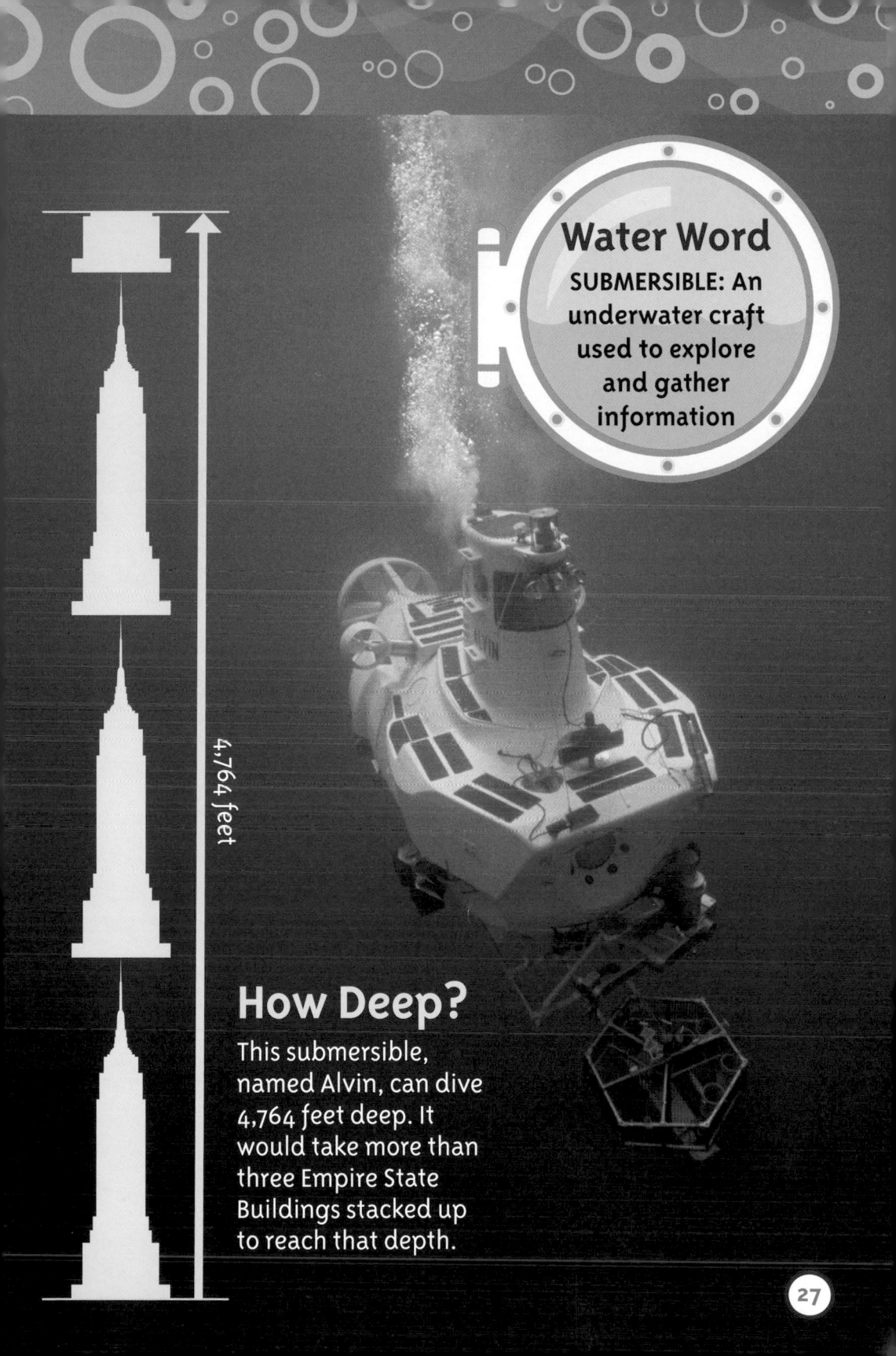


## Water Word

**SUBMERSIBLE:** An underwater craft used to explore and gather information

## How Deep?

This submersible, named Alvin, can dive 4,764 feet deep. It would take more than three Empire State Buildings stacked up to reach that depth.

These odd tube worms live on the bottom of the ocean. They can grow to be eight feet tall.

Q Which fish lights up at night?

A A starfish!

Submersibles collect information. They have lights and special tools. They take pictures, and they gather plants, rocks, and animals.

Scientists used submersibles to find the weird creatures shown here. And there are probably thousands more that have not been found yet.

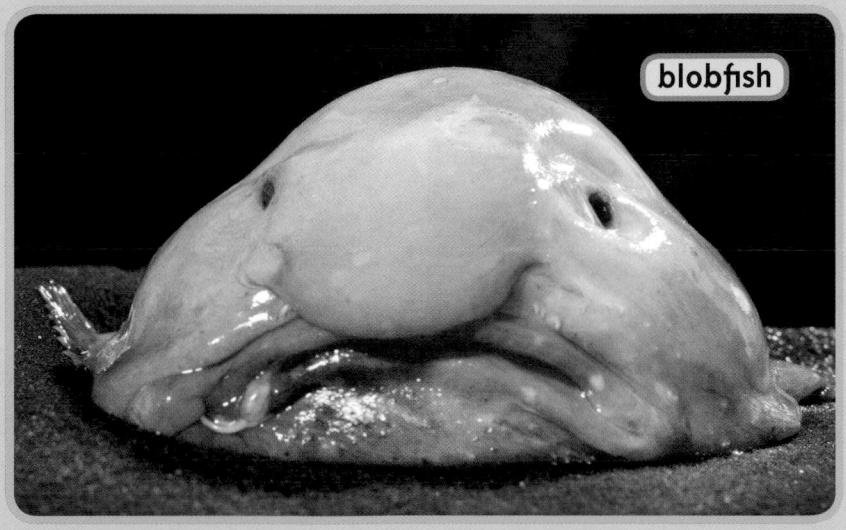

# Stump Your Parents

**Can your parents answer these questions about sea creatures? You might know more than they do!**

Answers are at the bottom of page 31.

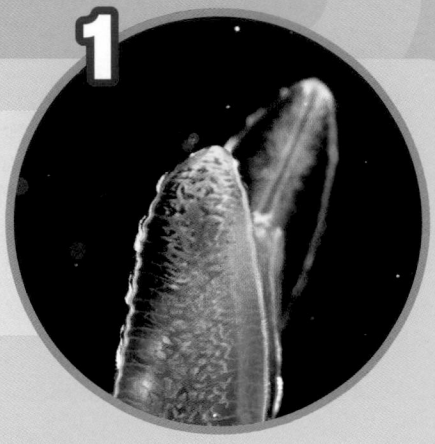

1

**Bioluminescence is ____.**

A. a loud sound
B. the light an animal makes
C. a search for food
D. a fast swim

2

**Machines that dive deep in the ocean are called ____.**

A. speedboats
B. planes
C. submersibles
D. scuba suits

3

**Which features are common in deep-sea animals?**

A. big mouth
B. big teeth
C. big eyes
D. all of the above

**Animals that have venom are ____.**

A. not harmful
B. friendly
C. able to cause stinging, pain, or death
D. only found in shallow waters

**Humans can't scuba dive deep into the ocean because ____.**

A. it's too cold
B. it's too dark
C. the pressure is too great
D. all of the above

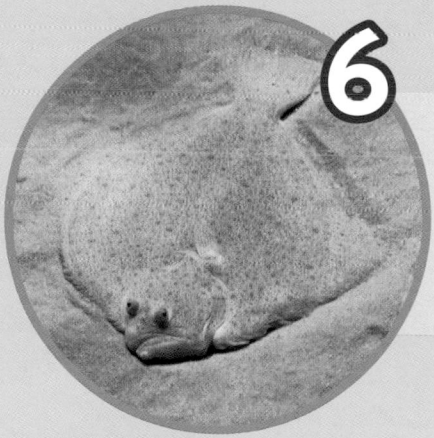

**What is camouflage?**

A. a way of eating
B. a way to blend in and hide
C. how animals see in the dark
D. none of the above

**An animal that is eaten by another animal is called ____.**

A. prey
B. an anemone
C. a tentacle
D. a creature

Answers: 1) B, 2) C, 3) D, 4) C, 5) D, 6) B, 7) A

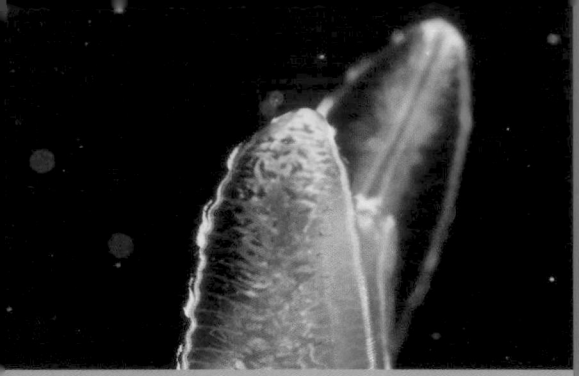

**BIOLUMINESCENCE:** Light that an animal makes by itself

**CAMOUFLAGE:** An animal's natural color or form that blends in with what is around it

**PREDATOR:** An animal that hunts and eats other animals

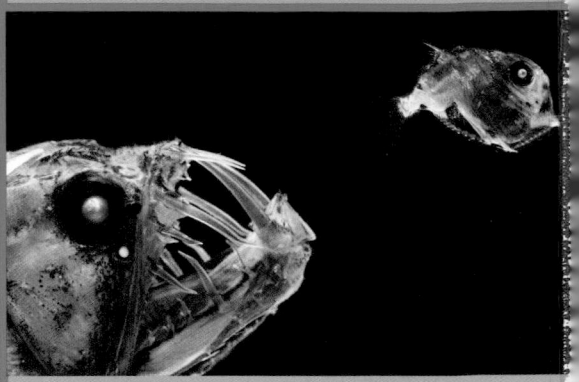

**PREY:** An animal that is eaten by another animal

**SUBMERSIBLE:** An underwater craft used to explore and gather information

**VENOM:** A liquid some animals make that can cause stinging, pain, or death